www.wadsworth.com

wadsworth.com is the World Wide Web site for Wadsworth and is your direct source to dozens of online resources.

At *www.wadsworth.com* you can find out about supplements, demonstration software, and student resources. You can also send email to many of our authors and preview new publications and exciting new technologies.

www.wadsworth.com
Changing the way the world learns®

Concept Charts
for Study and Review

to accompany

Psychology:
Themes and Variations

Briefer Version, Sixth Edition

Wayne Weiten

University of Nevada, Las Vegas

THOMSON ™

WADSWORTH

Australia • Canada • Mexico • Singapore • Spain • United Kingdom • United States

THOMSON

WADSWORTH

Psychology Editor: Michele Sordi
Development Editor: Jeremy Judson
Assistant Editor: Jennifer Keever
Editorial Assistant: Chelsea Junget
Technology Project Manager: Darin Derstine
Marketing Manager: Lori Grebe
Marketing Assistant: Laurel Anderson
Advertising Project Manager: Tami Strang
Project Manager, Editorial Production: Paula Berman
Art Director: Vernon T. Boes

Print Buyer: Karen Hunt
Permissions Editor: Linda L. Rill
Production Service: Thomas E. Dorsaneo
Copy Editor: Jackie Estrada
Cover Designer: Carole Lawson
Cover Image: ©WIDES + HOLL/Taxi/Getty Images
Text and Cover Printer: Transcontinental Printing/ Interglobe
Compositor: Thompson Type

Printed in Canada
1 2 3 4 5 6 7 08 07 06 05 04

ISBN: 0-534-63290-4

For more information about our products, contact us at:
Thomson Learning Academic Resource Center
1-800-423-0563
For permission to use material from this text or product, submit a request online at
http://www.thomsonrights.com
Any additional questions about permissions can be submitted by e-mail to
thomsonrights@thomson.com

Wadsworth/Thomson Learning
10 Davis Drive
Belmont, CA 94002-3098
USA

Asia
Thomson Learning
5 Shenton Way #01-01
UIC Building
Singapore 068808

Australia/New Zealand
Thomson Learning
102 Dodds Street
Southbank, Victoria 3006
Australia

Canada
Nelson
1120 Birchmount Road
Toronto, Ontario M1K 5G4
Canada

Europe/Middle East/Africa
Thomson Learning
High Holborn House
50/51 Bedford Row
London WC1R 4LR
United Kingdom

Latin America
Thomson Learning
Seneca, 53
Colonia Polanco
11560 Mexico D.F.
Mexico

Spain/Portugal
Paraninfo
Calle/Magallanes, 25
28015 Madrid, Spain

Contents

ON THE WEB

For additional resources on the topics covered in this text, visit the *Psychology: Themes and Variations* Web site, where you will find practice quizzes, tutorials, Web links, simulations, critical thinking activities, flash cards, interactive exercises, and suggested readings available through INFOTRAC.

http://psychology.wadsworth.com/weiten_themes_6e/

Concept Charts for Study and Review

to accompany

Psychology:
Themes and Variations

Briefer Version, Sixth Edition

A Letter to the Student

Greetings! This booklet of Concept Charts is intended to help you organize, assimilate, and master the main ideas contained in your textbook, *Psychology: Themes & Variations (Briefer Version)*. In the pages that follow, you will find a two-page Concept Chart for each chapter. The Concept Charts provide you with very detailed roadmaps of the key ideas found in the main body of each chapter.

How are the Concept Charts different from the Chapter Reviews found near the end of each chapter in the book? First, they are quite a bit more detailed. Second, they are presented in an outline format. Research suggests that outlines of reading assignments can enhance students' understanding and retention of textbook material. Third, we have used color-coded, hierarchically organized charts to create snapshots of the chapters that allow you to quickly see the relationships among ideas and sections. Seeing how it all fits together should help you to better understand each chapter. Moreover, research suggests that encoding information visually as well as verbally aids retention.

Generally, the charts are laid out to follow the order of presentation in the chapter, reading left to right and top to bottom. The color coding shows you at a glance which ideas go together. Groups of ideas that are related all have the same background color. Connecting lines are also used to make the links between various groups of ideas readily apparent, including hierarchical relationships. When boxes are connected by arrows, these arrows reflect the operation of causal or time-related sequences.

How should you use the Concept Charts? Here's what I suggest:
1. Before reading each chapter, look over the relevant Concept Chart to get a quick overview of what you will be reading about. This brief preview can help you to better assimilate the chapter's information as you read.
2. After you have read a chapter, review the Concept Chart once again to make sure you have registered all the key ideas.
3. Then study the chapter as you normally would, using the Study Guide, *PsykTrek*, Web study tools, or whatever else works for you.
4. When you feel that you have mastered the chapter content reasonably well, return to the Concept Chart and make sure that you understand how it all fits together.
5. Finally, wrap up by working to memorize the key ideas outlined in the Concept Chart.

I hope these visual maps of chapter content help you to master the material in your textbook. Good luck in your studying efforts.

Wayne Weiten

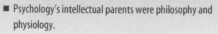

Chapter 1

The Evolution of Psychology

A new science is born

- Psychology's intellectual parents were philosophy and physiology.
- Psychology's founder was Wilhelm Wundt, who set up the first research lab in 1879 (in Germany).
- Wundt argued that psychology should be the scientific study of consciousness.

The battle of the schools begins

- Advocates of *structuralism* argued that psychology should use introspection to analyze consciousness into its basic elements.
- Advocates of *functionalism* argued that psychology should investigate the purposes of consciousness.
- Functionalism had a more lasting impact on psychology, as it fostered the emergence of behaviorism and applied psychology.

Evolutionary psychology gains prominence

- The 1990s saw the emergence of a major, new theoretical perspective called *evolutionary psychology*.
- Its crucial premise is that the patterns of behavior seen in a species are the product of evolution, just like anatomical characteristics.
- According to evolutionary psychologists, *natural selection* favors behaviors that enhance organisms' reproductive success.

Interest in cultural factors grows

- In the 1980s, Western psychologists developed increased interest in how cultural variables influence behavior.
- This trend was stimulated by the increased cultural diversity in Western societies and by growing global interdependence.

Cognition and physiology resurface

- In its early days, psychology emphasized the study of consciousness and physiology, but these topics languished as behaviorism grew more dominant.
- During the 1950s and 1960s advances in research on mental and physiological processes led to renewed interest in cognition and the biological bases of behavior.

Psychology becomes a profession

- In the first half of the 20th century, only a handful of psychologists were involved in the delivery of professional services to the public.
- However, stimulated by the demands of World War II, *clinical psychology* began rapid growth in the 1950s.
- Today, about two-thirds of psychologists work in professional specialties.

Behaviorism debuts

- *Behaviorism*, founded by John B. Watson, asserted that psychology should study only observable behavior.
- This view gradually took hold and psychology became the scientific study of behavior (instead of consciousness).
- The behaviorists stressed the importance of environment over heredity and pioneered animal research.

Specialties in Contemporary Psychology

Professional specialties

- Clinical psychology
- Counseling psychology
- Educational and school psychology
- Industrial and organizational psychology

Research areas

- Developmental psychology
- Social psychology
- Experimental psychology
- Physiological psychology
- Cognitive psychology
- Personality
- Psychometrics

Freud focuses on unconscious forces

- Although Sigmund Freud's views were controversial, they gradually became influential.
- *Psychoanalytic theory* emphasizes unconscious determinants of behavior and the importance of sexuality.
- According to Freud, the *unconscious* consists of thoughts that one is not aware of but that still influence one's behavior.

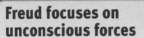

Behaviorism flourishes with the work of Skinner

- Boosted by B. F. Skinner's research, behaviorism reached its zenith of influence in the 1950s.
- Like Watson, he emphasized animal research, a strict focus on observable behavior, and the importance of environment.
- He generated controversy by arguing that free will is an illusion.

The humanists revolt

- Finding both behaviorism and psychoanalysis unappealing, advocates of *humanism*, such as Carl Rogers and Abraham Maslow, began to gain some influence in the 1950s.
- Humanism emphasizes the unique qualities of human behavior and the irrelevance of animal research.
- The humanists also took an optimistic view of human nature, stressing humans' freedom and potential for growth.

Key Themes

Themes related to psychology as a field of study

- **Psychology is empirical**—it is based on objective observations made through research.
- **Psychology is theoretically diverse**—a variety of perspectives are needed to enhance our understanding of behavior.
- **Psychology evolves in a sociohistorical context**—dense connections exist between what happens in psychology and what happens in society at large.

Themes related to psychology's subject matter

- **Behavior is determined by multiple causes**—complex causation is the rule and single-cause explanations are usually incomplete.
- **Behavior is shaped by cultural heritage**—cultural factors exert considerable influence over some aspects of behavior.
- **Heredity and environment jointly influence behavior**—nature and nurture interactively shape most behavioral traits.
- **People's experience of the world is highly subjective**—people tend to see what they expect to see and what they want to see.

Chapter 2

The Research Enterprise in Psychology

 The Scientific Approach

Goals

- Measurement and description
- Understanding and prediction
- Application and control

Steps in an investigation

1. Formulate a testable hypothesis
2. Select the method and design the study
3. Collect the data
4. Analyze the data and draw conclusions
5. Report the findings

Advantages

Clarity and precision yields better communication.

Intolerance of error yields more reliable data.

 Experimental Research

Elements

Independent variable (IV): Condition or event manipulated by experimenter

Dependent variable (DV): Aspect of behavior thought to be affected by independent variable

Experimental group: Participants who receive special treatment

Control group: Similar subjects who do not receive treatment given to experimental group

Extraneous variables: Factors besides IV that might affect DV, hence they need to be controlled

Variations

- Can have one group of subjects serve as their own control group.
- Can manipulate more than one independent variable in a study.
- Can use multiple dependent variables in a study.

Advantages and disadvantages

+ Permits conclusions about cause and effect relationships
− Manipulations and control often make experiments artificial
− Practical realities and ethical concerns make it impossible to conduct experiments on many issues

 Descriptive/Correlational Research

Correlation

Correlation exists when two variables are related to each other.

Types: *Positive* (variables covary in the same direction) or *negative* (variables covary in the opposite direction)

Correlation coefficient: Numerical index of degree of relationship between two variables

Strength: The closer the correlation to either −1.00 or +1.00, the stronger the relationship

Prediction: The stronger the correlation, the better one can predict

Causation: Correlation is not equivalent to causation

Examples of specific methods

Naturalistic observation: Careful, systematic observation, but no intervention with subjects

Case study: In-depth investigation of single participant, typically involving data from many sources

Survey: Questionnaires and interviews are used to gather information about specific aspects of particpants' behavior

Advantages and disadvantages

+ Broadens the scope of phenomena that psychologists can study (can explore issues that could not be examined with experimental methods)
− Cannot demonstrate that two variables are causally related

Common Flaws in Research

Sampling bias
Exists when a sample is not representative of the population

Placebo effects
Occur when particpants' expectations lead them to experience some change even though they receive empty or fake treatment

Distortions in self-report data
Result from problems, such as social desirability bias and response sets, that happen when participants give verbal accounts of their behavior

Experimenter bias
Occurs when a researcher's expectations or preferences about the outcome of a study influence the results obtained

Ethical Issues

The question of deception
Should researchers be permitted to mislead participants?

YES
- Otherwise, important issues could not be investigated.
- Empirical evidence suggests that deception is not harmful to subjects.

NO
- Deception is inherently immoral and may undermine participants' trust in others.
- Deceptive studies often create stress for subjects.

The question of animal research
Should researchers be permitted to subject animals to harmful or painful procedures?

YES
- Otherwise, important issues could not be investigated.
- Relatively little animal research involves pain or harm.

NO
- Animals are entitled to the same rights as humans.
- Animal studies are often trivial or may not apply to humans.

Key Themes
- Psychology is empirical.
- People's experience of the world is highly subjective.

Chapter 3

The Biological Bases of Behavior

Communication in the Nervous System

Key parts of the neuron

Soma: Cell body

Dendrites: Branching structures that receive signals from other cells

Axon: Fiber that carries signals away from soma to other cells

Myelin sheath: Insulating material that encases some axons

Terminal buttons: Small knobs at ends of axons that release neurotransmitters at synapses

The neural impulse

Resting potential: Neuron's stable, negative charge when inactive

Action potential: Voltage spike that travels along axon

Absolute refractory period: Brief time after action potential before another action potential can begin

All-or-none law: A neuron either fires or doesn't fire

Organization of the Nervous System

Central nervous system

Brain **Spinal cord**

Peripheral nervous system

Somatic nervous system: Nerves to voluntary muscles, sensory receptors

Autonomic nervous system: Nerves to heart, blood vessels, smooth muscles, glands

Afferent (incoming) nerves

Efferent (outgoing) nerves

Sympathetic division: Mobilizes bodily resources

Parasympathetic division: Conserves bodily resources

Brain and Behavior

Plasticity of the brain

The anatomical structure and functional organization of the brain is somewhat malleable

Hindbrain

Midbrain

Involved in locating things in space; dopamine synthesis

Forebrain

Cerebellum: Coordinates fine muscle movement, balance

Medulla: Regulates unconscious functions such as breathing and circulation

Pons: Involved in sleep and arousal

Thalamus: Relay center for cortex; distributes incoming sensory signals, except smell

Cerebrum: Handles complex mental activities, such as sensing, learning, thinking, planning

Limbic system: Loosely connected network that contributes to emotion, memory, motivation

Hypothalamus: Regulates basic biological needs, such as hunger, thirst, sex

Frontal lobes: Primary motor cortex

Prefrontal cortex: May house executive control system crucial to planning and organization

Parietal lobes: Primary somatosensory cortex

Temporal lobes: Primary auditory cortex

Occipital lobes: Primary visual cortex

Hippocampus: Contributes to memory

Amygdala: Involved in learning of fear responses

Neurotransmitters and behavior

Acetylcholine: Released by neurons that control skeletal muscles

Serotonin: Involved in the regulation of sleep and arousal and perhaps aggression; abnormal levels linked to depression

Dopamine: Abnormal levels linked to schizophrenia; dopamine circuits activated by cocaine and amphetamines

Norepinephrine: Abnormal levels linked to depression; norepinephrine circuits may be activated by cocaine and amphetamines

Endorphins: Involved in the modulation of pain

Synaptic transmission

Synthesis and storage of neurotransmitters in synaptic vesicles → **Release** of neurotransmitters into synaptic cleft → **Binding** of neurotransmitters at receptor sites lead to *excitatory and inhibitory PSPs* → **Inactivation or removal** (drifting away) of neurotransmitters

Reuptake of neurotransmitters by presynaptic neuron

Right Brain/Left Brain

Methods for study of lateralization

Split brain surgery: Bundle of fibers (corpus callosum) that connects two hemispheres is severed.

Perceptual asymmetries: Left-right imbalances in speed of processing are studied in normal subjects.

Left hemisphere
usually handles verbal processing, including language, speech, reading, writing

Right hemisphere
Usually handles nonverbal processing, including spatial, musical, and visual recognition tasks

Heredity and Behavior

Basic concepts

- Chromosomes are threadlike strands of DNA that carry information.
- Genes are DNA segments that are key functional units in hereditary transmission.
- Closer relatives share greater genetic overlap.
- Most behavioral traits appear to involve polygenic inheritance.

Research methods

Family studies assess trait resemblance among blood relatives.

Twin studies compare trait resemblance of identical and fraternal twins.

Adoption studies compare adopted children to their adoptive parents and to their biological parents.

Endocrine system

- Consists of glands that secrete chemicals called *hormones* into the bloodstream
- Among other things, hormones regulate sexual development and responses to stress

Evolutionary Bases of Behavior

Darwin's insights

1. Organisms vary in endless ways.
2. Some traits are heritable.
3. Variations in hereditary traits might affect organisms' survival and reproductive success.
4. Heritable traits that provide a survival or reproductive advantage will become more prevalent over generations (natural selection will change the gene pool of the population).

Key concepts

Fitness refers to the reproductive success of an organism relative to the population.

Adaptations are inherited characteristics sculpted through natural selection because they helped solve a problem of survival or reproduction when they emerged.

Behaviors as adaptive traits

- Species' typical patterns of behavior often reflect evolutionary solutions to adaptive problems.
- For example, behavioral strategies that help organisms avoid predators have obvious adaptive value.
- Many behavioral adaptations improve organisms' chances of reproductive success.

Key Themes

 Psychology is empirical.

 Heredity and environment jointly shape behavior.

 Behavior is determined by multiple causes.

Chapter 4

Sensation and Perception

The Visual System

Light waves

vary in | which affect perceptions of

Amplitude → Brightness

Wavelength → Color (hue)

Purity → Saturation

Light is registered by receptors in the eye

Key eye structures

include the

Lens, which focuses light rays falling on the retina

Pupil, which regulates the amount of light passing to the rear of the eye

Retina, which is the neural tissue lining the inside back surface of the eye

Optic disk, which is a hole in the retina that corresponds to the *blind spot*

Fovea, which is a tiny spot in the center of the retina where visual acuity is greatest

In the retina

Visual receptors

consist of *rods* and *cones,* which are organized into *receptive fields.*

Rods play a key role in night and peripheral vision and greatly outnumber cones.

Cones play a key role in day and color vision and provide greater acuity than rods.

Receptive fields are collections of rods and cones that funnel signals to specific visual cells in the retina or the brain.

Visual signals are sent onward to the brain

Visual pathways and processing

The main visual pathway projects through the thalamus, where visual signals are processed and distributed to areas in the occipital lobe.

The second visual pathway handles coordination of visual input with other sensory input.

The primary visual cortex in the *occipital lobe* handles the initial cortical processing of visual input.

Feature detectors are neurons in the visual cortex that respond selectively to specific features of complex stimuli.

After processing in the primary visual cortex, visual input is routed to other cortical areas along the *where pathway* (dorsal stream) and the *what pathway* (ventral stream).

Visual illusions

■ A *visual illusion* is a discrepancy between the appearance of a visual stimulus and its physical reality.

■ Visual illusions, such as the *Muller-Lyer illusion,* the *Ponzo illusion,* and the *moon illusion* show that perceptual hypotheses can be wrong and that perception is not a simple reflection of objective reality.

Color perception

Subtractive color mixing works by removing some wavelengths of light, leaving less light.

Additive color mixing works by putting more light in the mixture than any one light.

Trichromatic theory holds that the eye has three groups of receptors sensitive to wavelengths associated with red, green, and blue.

Opponent process theory holds that receptors make antagonistic responses to three pairs of colors.

Conclusion: The evidence suggests that both theories are necessary to explain color perception.

Form perception

■ The same visual input can result in very different perceptions.

■ Form perception is selective, as the phenomenon of *inattentional blindness* demonstrates.

■ Some aspects of form perception depend on *feature analysis,* which involves detecting specific elements and assembling them into complex forms.

■ *Gestalt principles,* such as *figure and ground, proximity, closure, similarity, simplicity,* and *continuity* help explain how scenes are organized into discrete forms.

■ Form perception often involves *perceptual hypotheses,* which are inferences about the forms that could be responsible for the stimuli sensed.

Depth perception

Binocular cues are clues about distance based on the differing views of the two eyes.

Retinal disparity, for example, refers to the fact that the right and left eyes see slightly different views of objects within 25 feet.

Monocular cues are clues about distance based on the image in either eye alone.

Pictorial cues are monocular cues that can be given in a flat picture, such as *linear perspective, texture gradients, relative size, height in plane, interposition,* and *light and shadow.*

The Auditory System

Sound waves

vary in   which affect perceptions of

Amplitude ⟶ Loudness

Wavelength ⟶ Pitch

Purity ⟶ Timbre

Sound is registered by receptors in the ear

Key ear structures

include the

Pinna, which is the external ear's sound-collecting cone

Eardrum, which is a taut membrane at the end of the auditory canal that vibrates in response to sound waves

Ossicles, which are three tiny bones in the middle ear that convert the eardrum's vibrations into smaller motions

Cochlea, which is the fluid-filled, coiled tunnel that houses the inner ear's neural tissue

Basilar membrane, which holds the hair cells that serve as auditory receptors

Pitch perception

Place theory holds that perception of pitch depends on the portion of the basilar membrane vibrated.

Frequency theory holds that perception of pitch depends on the basilar membrane's rate of vibration.

Conclusion: The evidence suggests that both theories are needed to explain pitch perception.

Other Senses

Taste

- Taste cells absorb chemicals in saliva and trigger neural impulses routed through the thalamus.
- Taste buds are sensitive to four basic tastes: sweet, sour, bitter and salty.
- Sensitivity to these tastes is distributed somewhat unevenly across the tongue, but the variations are small.
- Taste preferences are largely learned and heavily shaped by social processes.
- Super tasters have more taste buds and are more sensitive than others to certain sweet and bitter substances.

Smell

- Olfactory cilia absorb chemicals in the nose and trigger neural impulses.
- Smell is the only sensory system that is not routed through the thalamus.
- Most olfactory receptors respond to more than one odor.
- People tend to have a hard time attaching names to odors.

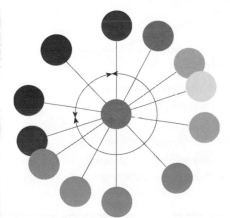

Touch

- Sensory receptors in the skin respond to pressure, temperature, and pain.
- Pain signals travel along a *fast pathway* that registers localized pain and a *slow pathway* that carries less localized pain sensations.
- Cultural variations in the experience of pain show the subjective nature of pain perception.
- *Gate-control theory* holds that incoming pain signals can be blocked in the spinal cord.
- Endorphins and a descending neural pathway appear responsible for this supression of pain.

Key Themes

- ⬡ Psychology is characterized by theoretical diversity.
- ⬢ People's experience of the world is highly subjective.
- ⬚ Behavior is shaped by one's cultural heritage.

Chapter 5

Variations in Consciousness

Consciousness

The nature of consciousness

- *Consciousness* involves varied levels of awareness.
- Mental processes continue during sleep, as some stimuli can penetrate awareness.
- Changes in consciousness are correlated with changes in brain activity as measured by the EEG.
- The evolutionary significance of consciousness is a matter of debate.

The architecture of sleep

- *Non-REM sleep* consists of stages 1–4, which are marked by an absence of rapid eye movements, relatively little dreaming, and varied EEG activity.
- *REM sleep* is a deep stage of sleep marked by rapid eye movements, high-frequency brain waves, and dreaming.
- During the course of sleep, REM periods gradually get longer and non-REM periods get shorter and shallower.

Sleep deprivation

Partial deprivation is common and can impair alertness and appears to contribute to many accidents.

REM deprivation leads to increased attempts to shift into REM and subsequent REM rebound.

Sleep

Biological Rhythms

Relations to sleep

- Circadian (24-hour) rhythms are influential in the regulation of sleep.
- Internal biological clocks are reset by exposure to light, which stimulates the SCN, which signals the pineal gland to secrete melatonin.
- The poor sleep associated with jet lag and rotating shift work is due to being out of sync with circadian rhythms.
- Administration of melatonin may have some value in reducing the effects of jet lag.

Factors influencing sleep

- The REM portion of sleep declines from 50% among newborns to about 20% among adults.
- The time spent in *slow-wave sleep* declines during adulthood.
- Culture does not appear to have much effect on the architecture of sleep.
- Culture does influence napping practices and co-sleeping, which is normative in many societies.

Sleep disorders

Insomnia refers to chronic problems in getting adequate sleep.

Narcolepsy is marked by sudden and irresistible onsets of sleep during normal waking periods.

Sleep apnea involves frequent, reflexive gasping for air that disrupts sleep.

Somnambulism (sleepwalking) occurs when a person wanders about while remaining asleep.

The World of Dreams

The nature of dreams

- Dreams are less exotic than widely assumed.
- Children's dreams are somewhat different from adults' dreams.
- Dreams may be affected by events in one's life and external stimuli.
- Cultural variations are seen in dream recall, dream content, dream interpretation, and the importance attributed to dreams.

Theories of dreaming

- Sigmund Freud asserted that the chief purpose of dreams is wish fulfillment.
- Other theorists argue that dreams provide an opportunity to think creatively about personal problems.
- The *activation-synthesis model* proposes that dreams are side effects of the neural activation that produces waking-like brain waves during REM sleep.

Hypnosis

Hypnotic induction and phenomena

- *Hypnosis* is a procedure that produces a heightened state of suggestibility.
- People vary in their susceptibility to hypnosis.
- Hypnosis can produce a variety of effects, including anesthesia, sensory distortions, disinhibition, and posthypnotic amnesia.

Theories of hypnosis

- According to Theodore Barber, hypnosis produces a normal state of consciousness in which people act out the role of hypnotized subject.
- The *role-playing view* is supported by evidence that hypnotic feats can be duplicated by nonhypnotized subjects and that hypnotic subjects are often acting out a role.
- According to Ernest Hilgard, hypnosis produces an altered state of awareness characterized by dissociation.
- The *altered state view* is supported by evidence that divided consciousness is a common state that has continuity with everyday experience.

Meditation

Physiological correlates and long-term benefits

- Meditation refers to a family of practices that train attention to heighten awareness and bring mental processes under greater voluntary control.
- Studies suggest that effective meditation leads to a beneficial physiological state that may be accompanied by changes in brain activity.
- Studies suggest that meditation may have a variety of long-term benefits, but critics argue that most of these benefits are simply a byproduct of effective relaxation.

Altering Consciousness with Drugs

Principal abused drugs

Narcotics are drugs derived from opium, such as heroin.

Sedatives are sleep-inducing drugs, such as barbiturates.

Stimulants are drugs that increase CNS activation, such as cocaine and amphetamines.

Hallucinogens, such as LSD and mescaline, produce sensory distortions and diverse mental and emotional effects.

Cannabis is the hemp plant from which marijuana, hashish, and THC are derived.

Alcohol includes a variety of beverages that contain ethyl alcohol.

MDMA (ecstasy) is a compound drug related to amphetamines and hallucinogens.

Factors influencing drug effects

- Drug effects depend on users' age, mood, personality, weight, expectations, and previous experience with drugs.
- Drug effects also depend on the potency of the drug, the method of administration, and the user's tolerance.

Risks associated with drug abuse

- *Physical dependence* exists when drug use must be continued to avoid withdrawal illness.
- *Psychological dependence* exists when drug use must be continued to satisfy craving for the drug.
- Many drugs, especially CNS depressants, can produce a lethal *overdose*.
- Many drugs cause deleterious health effects by producing *direct tissue damage*.
- The negative effects of drugs on physical health are often due to *indirect behavioral effects*.

Mechanisms of drug action

- Psychoactive drugs exert their effects by selectively altering neurotransmitter activity.
- Increased activation in the *mesolimbic dopamine pathway* may be responsible for the reinforcing effects of many drugs.

Key Themes

- Psychology is characterized by theoretical diversity.
- People's experience of the world is highly subjective.
- Behavior is shaped by one's cultural heritage.
- Psychology evolves in a sociohistorical context.

Chapter 6

Learning

Classical Conditioning

Operant Conditioning

Description

- *Classical conditioning* is a type of learning in which a stimulus acquires the capacity to evoke a response originally evoked by another stimulus.
- Classical conditioning was pioneered by Ivan Pavlov, who conditioned dogs to salivate when a tone was presented.
- Classical conditioning mainly regulates involuntary, reflexive responses.
- Examples include emotional responses (such as fears) and physiological responses (such as immunosuppression).

- *Operant conditioning* is a type of learning in which responses come to be controlled by their consequences.
- Operant conditioning was pioneered by B. F. Skinner, who showed that rats and pigeons tend to repeat responses that are followed by favorable outcomes.
- Operant conditioning mainly regulates voluntary, spontaneous responses.
- Examples include studying, going to work, telling jokes, asking someone out, and gambling.

Terminology and procedures

- Responses controlled through classical conditioning are said to be *elicited*.
- Classical conditioning begins with an *unconditioned stimulus (UCS)* that elicits an *unconditioned response (UCR)*.
- Then a neutral stimulus is paired with the UCS until it becomes a *conditioned stimulus (CS)* that elicits a *conditioned response (CR)*.

- Responses controlled through operant conditioning are said to be *emitted*.
- Demonstrations of operant conditioning typically occur in a *Skinner box* where an animal's reinforcement is controlled.
- The key dependent variable is the animal's *response rate* as monitored by a *cumulative recorder*, with results portrayed in graphs (steeper slopes are indicative of faster responding).

Basic processes

Acquisition is the formation of a conditioned response tendency.

Extinction is the gradual weakening of a conditioned response tendency.

Generalization occurs when an organism responds to new stimuli besides the original stimulus.

Discrimination occurs when an organism does not respond to other stimuli that resemble the original stimulus.

- *Acquisition* occurs when a CS and UCS are paired, gradually resulting in a CR.
- Acquistion depends on *stimulus contiguity*, which is a temporal association between events.
- *Extinction* occurs when a CS is repeatedly presented alone until it no longer elicits a CR.
- *Spontaneous recovery* is the reappearance of an extinguished response after a period of nonexposure to the CS.
- *Generalization* occurs when a CR is elicited by a new stimulus that resembles the original CS, as in Watson and Rayner's study of Little Albert.
- *Discrimination* occurs when a CR is not elicited by a new stimulus that resembles the original CS.
- *Higher-order conditioning* occurs when a CS functions as if it were a UCS.

- *Acquisition* occurs when a response gradually increases due to contingent reinforcement.
- Acquistion may involve *shaping*—the reinforcement of closer and closer approximations of the desired response.
- *Extinction* occurs when responding gradually slows and stops after reinforcement is terminated.
- *Resistance to extinction* occurs when an organism continues to make a response after reinforcement for it has been terminated.
- *Generalization* occurs when responding increases in the presence of a stimulus that resembles the original discriminative stimulus.
- *Discrimination* occurs when responding does not increase in the presence of a stimulus that resembles the original discriminative stimulus.
- *Primary reinforcers* are inherently reinforcing, whereas *secondary reinforcers* develop through learning.

Schedules of reinforcement

- *Intermittent reinforcement* occurs when a response is reinforced only some of the time.
- In *ratio schedules*, the reinforcer is given after a fixed (FR) or variable (VR) number of nonreinforced responses.
- In *interval schedules*, the reinforcer is given for the first response that occurs after a fixed (FI) or variable (VI) time interval has elapsed.
- Ratio schedules (FR and VR) tend to yield higher response rates, whereas variable schedules (VR and VI) tend to yield more resistance to extinction.

Distinctions among operant outcomes

- *Positive reinforcement* occurs when a response is followed by the presentation of a rewarding stimulus.
- *Negative reinforcement* occurs when a response is followed by the removal of an aversive stimulus.
- Negative reinforcement plays a key role in *escape learning* and *avoidance learning*.
- *Punishment* occurs when an event following a response weakens the tendency to make that response.
- Punishment may result in side effects such as negative emotional responses and increased aggressive behavior.
- When used for disciplinary reasons, punishment should be: applied swiftly, just severe enough to be effective, explained, and not physical.

New Directions in the Study of Conditioning

Recognizing biological constraints on learning

- *Instinctive drift* occurs when an animal's innate response tendencies interfere with conditioning processes.
- John Garcia found that it is almost impossible to create some associations, whereas *conditioned taste aversions* are readily acquired in spite of long CS-UCS delays, which he attributed to evolutionary influences.
- Differences in the adaptive challenges faced by various species have probably led to some species-specific learning tendencies.

Recognizing cognitive processes in conditioning

- Robert Rescorla showed that the predictive value of a CS influences the process of classical conditioning.
- When a response is followed by a desirable outcome, the response is more likely to be strengthened if it appears to have caused the favorable outcome.
- Modern theories hold that conditioning is a matter of detecting the contingencies that govern events.

Observational Learning

- *Observational learning* occurs when an organism's responding is influenced by the observation of others, called *models*.
- Observational learning was pioneered by Albert Bandura, who showed that conditioning does not have to be a product of direct experience.
- Both classical and operant conditioning can take place through observational learning.
- Observational learning can explain why physical punishment tends to *increase* aggression in children even when it is intended to do the opposite.

Key Themes

- Heredity and environment interactively govern behavior.
- Psychology evolves in a sociohistorical context.

Chapter 7

Human Memory

 Encoding

 Storage

 Retrieval

- *Attention,* which entails a selective focus on certain input, enhances encoding.
- *Divided attention* undermines encoding and can have a negative effect on the performance of other tasks.
- *Levels-of-processing theory* proposes that deeper levels of processing result in more durable memory codes.
- *Structural, phonemic,* and *semantic encoding* represent progressively deeper levels of processing.
- *Elaboration* and *visual imagery* can enrich encoding.

- Information-processing theories propose that people have three memory stores: *sensory memory, short-term memory (STM),* and *long-term memory (LTM).*
- Atkinson and Shiffrin posited that incoming information passes through two temporary storage buffers before being placed into long-term memory.
- The three memory stores are not viewed as anatomical structures but as distinct types of memory.

- Recall is often guided by partial information, as demonstrated by the *tip-of-the tongue phenomenon.*
- Reinstating the context of an event can often enhance retrieval efforts.
- Memories are sketchy reconstructions of the past that may be distorted.
- The *misinformation effect* occurs when recall of an event is changed by misleading postevent information.
- A *source-monitoring error* occurs when a memory derived from one source is attributed to another source.

Sensory memory

- Sensory memory preserves information in its original form for a very brief time.
- Memory traces in the sensory store appear to decay in about one-quarter of a second.

Short-term memory

- Short-term memory can maintain about seven chunks of unrehearsed information for up to 20 seconds.
- *Working memory* is a four-component model of short-term memory that views it as more than a rehearsal buffer.

Long-term memory

- Long-term memory is an unlimited capacity store that can hold information indefinitely.
- Flashbulb memories suggest that LTM storage may be permanent, but the data are not convincing.
- Memories can be organized in a variety of ways.

Organization in long-term memory

Schemas

A *schema* is an organized cluster of information about an object or event.

Semantic networks

A *semantic network* consists of concepts joined by pathways linking related concepts.

Connectionist networks

PDP models assume that memories consist of patterns of activation in *connectionist networks* that resemble neural networks.

Forgetting

Why we forget

- A great deal of forgetting, including pseudoforgetting, is due to *ineffective encoding*.
- *Decay theory* proposes that memory traces fade with time, but decay does not appear to be a factor in long-term memory.
- *Interference theory* asserts that people forget information because of competition from other material, which has proven easy to demonstrate.
- Forgetting is often due to *retrieval failure*, which may include repression.

Measuring forgetting

- Ebbinghaus's work suggested that most forgetting occurs very rapidly, but subsequent research indicated that his *forgetting curve* was exceptionally steep.
- Retention can be assessed with a *recall* measure, a *recognition* measure, or a *relearning* measure.

The repressed memories controversy

- Recent years have seen a surge of reports of recovered memories of previously forgotten sexual abuse in childhood.
- Many clinicians accept these recovered memories, arguing that it is common for people to bury traumatic memories in their unconscious.
- Many memory researchers are skeptical of recovered memories because they have demonstrated that it is easy to create inaccurate memories in laboratory studies.
- Although it is clear that some therapists have created false memories in their patients, it seems likely that some cases of recovered memories are authentic.

Physiology of Memory

Anatomy of memory

The study of amnesia and other research has suggested that the hippocampal region may play a key role in the consolidation of memories.

Neural circuitry of memory

Some theorists believe that memories may correspond to localized neural pathways in the brain.

Biochemistry of memory

Some theorists argue that memories may correspond to alterations in neurotransmitter activity at specific synapses.

Proposed Memory Systems

Explicit memory

- *Explicit memory* involves intentional recollection of previous experiences.
- Explicit memory is conscious, accessed directly, and best assessed with recall or recognition measures of retention.

Observed memory phenomena

Implicit memory

- *Implicit memory* is apparent when retention is exhibited on a task that does not require intentional remembering.
- Implicit memory is unconscious, accessed indirectly, and best assessed with relearning measures of retention.

Declarative memory

The *declarative memory system* handles recall of factual information, such as names, dates, events, and ideas.

Underlying memory systems

Procedural memory

The *procedural memory system* handles recall of actions, skills, and operations, such as riding a bike or typing.

Semantic memory

The *semantic memory system* contains general knowledge that is not temporally dated.

Episodic memory

The *episodic memory system* handles temporally dated recollections of personal experiences.

Key Themes

- People's experience of the world is highly subjective.
- Behavior is determined by multiple causes.
- Psychology is characterized by theoretical diversity.

Chapter 8

Cognition and Intelligence

 **Problem Solving**

Types of problems

Greeno has distinguished between problems of inducing structure, problems of arrangement, and problems of transformation.

Barriers to problem solving

- People are often distracted by irrelevant information.

- *Functional fixedness* is the tendency to perceive an item only in terms of its most common use.

- A *mental set* exists when people persist in using strategies that have worked in the past but are no longer optimal.

- People often impose unnecessary constraints on their possible solutions.

Approaches to problem solving

- *Trial and error* is a common, albeit primitive, approach to problem solving.

- A *heuristic* is a rule of thumb or mental shortcut used in solving problems or making decisions.

- It is often useful to formulate intermediate subgoals.

- If you can spot an analogy between one problem and another, a solution may become apparent.

- When progress is stalled, changing the representation of a problem often helps.

Culture and problem solving

- *Field dependence* involves reliance on external frames of reference, whereas *field independence* involves reliance on internal frames of reference.

- Culture influences whether people become field dependent or independent.

- People who are field independent tend to analyze and restructure problems more than field dependent people do.

- Research suggests that Eastern cultures exhibit a more holistic cognitive style, whereas Western cultures display a more analytic cognitive style.

 Decision Making

Basic strategies

- Herbert Simon's *theory of bounded rationality* asserts that people tend to use simple decision strategies that often yield seemingly irrational results because they can only juggle so much information at once.

- An *additive decision model* is used when people rate the attributes of alternatives and select the option with the highest sum.

- *Elimination by aspects* involves gradually ruling out alternatives that fail to satisfy minimum criteria.

- When decisions involve few options and attributes, people tend to favor additive strategies, but when options get complex, people tend to favor elimination by aspects.

- When people make risky decisions, they weigh the expected value and subjective utility of various outcomes.

Common heuristics and flaws

- The *availability heuristic* involves basing the estimated probability of an event on the ease with which relevant instances come to mind.

- The *representativeness heuristic* involves basing the estimated probability of an event on how similar it is to the typical prototype of that event.

- In estimating probabilities, people often ignore information on the *base rates* of events or are victimized by the *conjunction fallacy*.

- Decision makers also tend to fall victim to the *gambler's fallacy* and the *law of small numbers* (putting too much faith in small samples).

- People frequently overestimate the likelihood of improbable events, and they tend to be overconfident about their decisions.

- Evolutionary psychologists assert that people perform poorly in cognitive research because it presents them with contrived, artificial problems that do not involve natural categories and have no adaptive significance.

- According to Gerd Gigerenzer, people mostly depend on *fast and frugal heuristics* that are much simpler than the complicated inferential processes studied in traditional cognitive research.

Key Themes

- Psychology is empirical.
- Psychology evolves in a sociohistorical context.
- Heredity and environment jointly shape behavior.
- People's experience of the world is highly subjective.
- Behavior is shaped by one's cultural heritage.

Measuring Intelligence

History of intelligence tests

- Modern intelligence testing was launched in 1905 by Alfred Binet, who devised a scale to measure a child's mental age.

- Lewis Terman revised the Binet scale to produce the Stanford-Binet in 1916, which introduced the *intelligence quotient (IQ)*.

- In 1939, David Wechsler published an improved measure of intelligence for adults, which introduced the *deviation IQ score* based on the normal distribution.

Essentials of intelligence testing

- Intelligence tests contain a diverse mixture of questions that tap abstract reasoning skills.

- Modern deviation IQ scores indicate where people fall in the normal distribution of intelligence for their age.

- Individuals' IQ scores can vary across testings, but intelligence tests tend to have very high reliability.

- There is ample evidence that IQ tests are valid measures of academic/verbal intelligence, but they do not tap social or practical intelligence.

- IQ scores are correlated with occupational attainment, but doubts have been raised about how well they predict performance within a specific occupation.

- IQ tests are not widely used in most non-Western cultures.

Heredity and Environment as Determinants of Intelligence

Evidence for hereditary influence

- *Twin studies* show that identical twins are more similar in intelligence than fraternal twins, suggesting that intelligence is at least partly inherited.

- Even more impressive, identical twins reared apart are more similar in intelligence than fraternal twins reared together.

- Studies also show that adopted children resemble their biological parents in intelligence.

- A *heritability ratio* is an estimate of the proportion of trait variability in a population that is determined by genetic variations.

- Estimates of the heritability of intelligence mostly range from 50% to 70%, but heritability ratios have certain limitations.

Evidence for environmental influence

- *Adoption studies* find that adopted children show some IQ resemblance to their foster parents and to their adoptive siblings.

- Studies of *environmental deprivation* show that children raised in substandard circumstances tend to exhibit a gradual decline in IQ as they grow older.

- Generational increases in measured IQ are perplexing, but they must be due to environmental changes.

The interaction of heredity and environment

- The evidence clearly shows that intelligence is shaped by both heredity and environment and that these influences interact.

- The *reaction range model* posits that heredity sets limits on one's intelligence and that environmental factors determine where people fall within these limits.

 New Directions

- Although recent years have brought increased interest in biological indexes of intelligence, relatively little progress has been made.

- Robert Sternberg's triarchic theory posits that the hallmarks of intelligence are the abilities to deal with novelty and handle familiar tasks automatically.

- According to Sternberg, successful intelligence includes three facets: analytical intelligence, creative intelligence, and practical intelligence.

- Howard Gardner has argued that there are eight largely independent types of human intelligence.

The debate about cultural differences in IQ scores

- Arthur Jensen and others have argued that cultural differences in IQ scores are largely due to heredity.

- Even if the heritability of IQ is high, group differences in IQ could be entirely environmental in origin.

- Socioeconomic disadvantage may contribute to cultural differences in IQ.

Chapter 9

Motivation and Emotion

Motivational Theories and Concepts

- *Drive theories* emphasize how *internal* states of tension (due to disruptions of homeostasis) *push* organisms in certain directions.

- *Incentive theories* emphasize how *external* goals *pull* organisms in certain directions.

- *Evolutionary theories* assert that motives are a product of *natural selection* that have had adaptive value in terms of fostering reproductive fitness.

- Most theories of motivation distinguish between *biological motives* originating in bodily needs and *social motives* originating in social experiences.

Motivation of Hunger

Biological factors regulating hunger

- Research orginally suggested that the *lateral* and *ventromedial areas of the hypothalamus* were the brain's on-off switches for hunger, but the dual-centers model proved too simple.

- Today, scientists think that *neural circuits* passing through the hypothalamus play a larger role in the regulation of hunger.

- Fluctuations in blood glucose monitored by *glucostats* also influence hunger.

- In the digestive system, the stomach can send two types of satiety signals to the brain.

- Secretions of the pancreatic hormone *insulin* are associated with increased hunger.

- The recently discovered hormone *leptin* provides the hypothalamus with information about the body's fat stores.

Environmental factors regulating hunger

- Incentive-oriented theorists emphasize that the *availability* and *palatability* of food are key factors influencing hunger.

- Hunger can be triggered by food cues in the environment, such as odors.

- Humans show some innate taste preferences, but learning is much more influential.

- Classical conditioning and observational learning shape what people prefer to eat.

- Food preferences are also governed by exposure, which is why there are huge cultural variations in eating habits.

- Stressful events can elicit arousal and heightened arousal is associated with overeating.

Sexual Motivation

The human sexual response

Masters and Johnson showed that the sexual response cycle consists of four stages: excitement, plateau, orgasm, and resolution.

Sexual orientation

- People tend to view heterosexuality and homosexuality as an all-or-none distinction, but it is more accurate to view them as endpoints on a continuum.

- Environmental explanations of sexual orientation have not been supported by research.

- Biological explanations have fared better in recent years, as twin studies have shown that genetic factors influence sexual orientation.

- Research also suggests that idiosyncrasies in prenatal hormonal secretions may influence sexual orientation.

Evolutionary analyses

- According to *parental investment theory,* the sex that makes the smaller investment in offspring will compete for mating opportunities with the sex that makes the larger investment, which will be more discriminating in selecting partners.

- Human males are required to invest little in offspring, so their reproductive potential is maximized by mating with as many partners as possible.

- Human females have to invest months to years in carrying and nourishing offspring, so they maximize their reproductive potential by mating with males who are able to invest more resources in their offspring.

Gender differences in sexual activity

- Males think about sex and initiate sex more often than females.

- Males are more willing to engage in casual sex and have more partners than females.

Gender differences in mate preferences

- Males around the world place more emphasis than females on potential partners' youthfulness and attractiveness.

- Females around the world place more emphasis than males on partners' intelligence and financial prospects.

Physiological component

- The physiological component of emotion is dominated by autonomic arousal.
- A *polygraph* detects emotional arousal, which is a far from perfect index of lying.
- According to Joseph LeDoux, the amygdala lies at the core of a complex set of neural circuits that process emotion.

Cognitive component

- The cognitive component of emotion consists of subjective feelings that are often intense and difficult to control.
- Cognitive appraisals of events influence the emotions that people experience.

Behavioral component

- At the behavioral level, emotions are revealed through body language.
- People can identify at least six emotions based on facial expressions.
- According to the *facial-feedback hypothesis,* facial muscles send signals to the brain that aid in the recognition of emotions.

Emotion

Cultural considerations

- Ekman and Friesen have found cross-cultural agreement in the identification of emotions based on facial expressions.
- Cross-cultural similarities have also been found in the cognitive and physiological components of emotion.
- However, there are cultural disparities in how emotions are categorized and in public displays of emotions.

Theoretical views

- The *James-Lange theory* asserted that the conscious experience of emotion results from one's perception of autonomic arousal.
- The *Cannon-Bard theory* asserted that emotions originate in subcortical areas of the brain.
- According to the *two-factor theory,* people infer emotion from autonomic arousal and then label it in accordance with their cognitive explanation for the arousal.
- *Evolutionary theories of emotion* assert that emotions are innate reactions that do not depend on cognitive processes.

Fear

Achievement Motivation

- David McClelland pioneered the use of the TAT to measure individual differences in *need for achievement*.
- People who score high in the need for achievement tend to work harder and more persistently than others and are more likely to delay gratification.
- However, people high in the need for achievement tend to choose challenges of intermediate difficulty.
- The pursuit of achievement goals tends to increase when the probability of success on a task and the incentive value of success are higher.

Key Themes

- Psychology is theoretically diverse.
- Psychology evolves in a sociohistorical context.
- Heredity and environment jointly influence behavior.
- Behavior is shaped by cultural heritage.
- Behavior is determined by multiple causes.

Chapter 10

Human Development Across the Life Span

Prenatal Development

Stages

- During the *germinal stage* a zygote becomes a mass of cells that implants in the uterine wall and the *placenta* begins to form.
- During the *embryonic stage* most vital organs and bodily systems begin to form, making it a period of great vulnerability.
- During the *fetal stage* organs continue to grow and gradually begin to function, as the fetus reaches the *age of viability* around 22–26 weeks.

Environmental influences

- Maternal malnutrition increases newborns' risk for birth complications and neurological deficits.
- Maternal consumption of alcohol, tobacco, and other drugs can have a variety of negative effects on prenatal development.
- Maternal illnesses can interfere with prenatal development, and genital herpes and AIDS can be passed to newborns at birth.

Motor development

- Motor development follows *cephalocaudal* (head-to-foot) and *proximodistal* (center-outward) trends.
- Early progress in motor skills has traditionally been attributed to *maturation,* but recent research suggests that infants' exploration is also important.
- Cross-cultural research on motor development shows that maturation and environment are both influential.

Language development

- Starting at around 6 months, infants' *babbling* increasingly resembles the language spoken in the child's environment.
- Children typically utter their first words around their first birthday.
- Vocabulary growth is slow at first, but *fast mapping* contributes to a *vocabulary spurt* that often begins at around 18–24 months.
- Children begin to combine words by the end of their second year, exhibiting *telegraphic speech.*
- Children's sentences gradually increase in length, but their grammar is often marked by *overregularizations.*

Attachment

- *Attachment* emerges out of a complex interplay between infant and mother.
- Research by Mary Ainsworth showed that infant-mother attachments fall into three categories: secure, anxious-ambivalent, and avoidant.
- Cultural variations in child rearing influence the patterns of attachment seen in a society.

Cognitive development

- Jean Piaget proposed that children evolve through four stages of cognitive development.
- The major achievement of the *sensorimotor period* (birth to age 2) is the development of object permanence.
- Children's thought during the *preoperational period* (ages 2–7) is marked by centration, animism, irreversibility, and egocentrism.
- In the *concrete operational period* (ages 7-11) children develop the ability to perform operations on mental representations.
- In the *formal operational period* (age 11 onward) thought becomes more systematic, abstract and logical.
- Researchers have found that infants understand complex concepts, such as addition, that they have had little opportunity to acquire through learning.
- Nativists and evolutionary theorists argue that children's brains are prewired to readily understand certain concepts.

Development in Childhood

Moral development

- Lawrence Kohlberg's theory proposes that individuals progress through three levels of moral reasoning.
- *Preconventional reasoning* focuses on acts' consequences, *conventional reasoning* on the need to maintain social order, and *postconventional reasoning* on working out a personal code of ethics.
- Age-related progress in moral reasoning has been found in research, but there is a lot of overlap among stages.

Personality development

- Erik Erikson's theory proposes that individuals evolve through eight stages over the life span.
- *Stage theories* assume that individuals progress through stages in a particular order, that progress is strongly related to age, and that new stages bring major changes in characteristic behavior.
- Erikson's four childhood stages are trust versus mistrust, autonomy versus shame, initiative versus guilt, and industry versus inferiority.

Development in Adolescence

Puberty and the growth spurt

- Brought on by hormonal changes, the *adolescent growth spurt* typically begins at about age 11 in girls and age 13 in boys.
- *Puberty* is the stage during which *primary sex characteristics* develop fully.
- Girls who reach puberty early and boys who mature relatively late have a greater risk for psychological and social difficulties.

Time of turmoil?

- Suicides and especially *attempted* suicides have risen dramatically among adolescents in recent decades, but *completed* suicide rates remain lower for adolescents than for older age groups.
- The data on *adolescent violence* suggest that adolescence is a time of turmoil, although the incidence of school violence has remained lower than widely perceived.
- The recent consensus of experts has been that adolescence does not appear to be more stressful than other periods of life.
- However, Jeffrey Arnett has marshalled evidence that suggests that adolescence is *somewhat* more stressful than other life stages.

The search for identity

- According to Erikson, the main challenge of adolescence is the struggle for a sense of identity.
- According to James Marcia, adolescents deal with their identity crisis in four ways: *foreclosure*, *moratorium*, *identity diffusion*, and *identity achievement*.
- Age trends in identity status generally are consistent with Marcia's theory, but there is great variability and most people reach identity achievement at later ages than originally envisioned.

Personality development

- During adulthood, personality generally remains fairly stable, but some people do experience significant changes.
- For the most part, research has not supported the notion that most people go through a *midlife crisis*.
- According to Erikson, people evolve through three stages of development in the adult years: intimacy versus isolation, generativity versus self-absorption, and integrity versus despair.

Development in Adulthood

Family transitions

- Adjusting to marriage is more likely to be difficult when spouses have different expectations about marital roles.
- Marital satisfaction tends to decline in the early years of marriage and to gradually climb later in the family life cycle.
- Parent-adolescent relations are not as contentious as widely assumed, but conflicts do increase and parents tend to feel stressed.
- For many parents the transition to an *empty nest* seems to be less difficult than it used to be.

Physical changes

- In the sensory domain, vision and hearing acuity tend to decline, but glasses and hearing aids can compensate for these losses.
- Women's reactions to menopause vary and menopause is not as stressful as widely believed.
- Brain tissue and weight tend to decline after age 60, but this loss does not appear to be the key to age-related dementias.
- *Dementias* are seen in about 15%-20% of people over age 75, but they are not part of the normal aging process.
- Alzheimer's patients exhibit profound loss of brain tissue and the accumulation of characteristic neural abnormalities.

Cognitive changes

- General intelligence is fairly stable throughout most of adulthood, with a small decline in average scores seen after age 60.
- The memory losses associated with aging are moderate and may be mostly due to declining working memory.
- Speed in cognitive processing tends to begin a gradual decline during middle adulthood.

Key Themes

- Psychology is theoretically diverse.
- Psychology evolves in a sociohistorical context.
- Heredity and environment jointly influence behavior.
- Behavior is shaped by cultural heritage.
- Behavior is determined by multiple causes.

Chapter 11

The Nature of Personality

- A *personality trait* is a durable disposition to behave in a particular way across a variety of situations.
- Theorists agree that some traits are more basic than others, but there is great debate about how many fundamental traits are required to fully describe personality.
- According to the *five-factor model*, most aspects of personality are derived from five crucial traits: neuroticism, extraversion, openness to experience, agreeableness, and conscientiousness.

 # Psychodynamic Perspectives

Freud's theory

- Sigmund Freud's *psychoanalytic theory* grew out of his therapeutic work with clients and emphasized the importance of the unconscious.
- Freud divided personality structure into three components: the id, ego, and superego.
- The *id* is the instinctive component that follows the pleasure principle, the *ego* is the decision-making component that follows the reality principle, and the *superego* is the moral component.
- Freud described three levels of awareness: the *conscious* (current awareness), the *preconscious* (material just beneath the surface of awareness), and the *unconscious* (material well below the surface of awareness).
- Freud theorized that conflicts centering on sex and aggression are especially likely to lead to significant anxiety.
- According to Freud, anxiety and other unpleasant emotions are often warded off with *defense mechanisms*, which work through self-deception.
- Freud proposed that children evolve through five stages of psychosexual development: the oral, anal, phallic, latency, and genital stages.
- Certain experiences during these stages, such as the handling of the *Oedipal complex*, can shape subsequent adult personality.

Jung's theory

- Carl Jung's *analytical psychology* emphasized unconscious determinants of personality, but he divided the unconscious into the personal and collective unconscious.
- The *collective unconscious* is a storehouse of latent memory traces inherited from people's ancestral past.
- These memories consist of *archetypes,* which are emotionally charged thought forms that have universal meaning.

Adler's theory

- Alfred Adler's *individual psychology* emphasized how social forces shape personality development.
- Adler argued that the *striving for superiority* is the foremost motivational force in people's lives.
- Adler attributed personality disturbances to excessive inferiority feelings that can pervert the normal process of striving for superiority and can result in overcompensation.

 # Behavioral Perspectives

Skinner's theory

- B. F. Skinner's work on *operant conditioning* was not meant to be a theory of personality, but it has been applied to personality.
- Skinner's followers view personality as a collection of response tendencies that are tied to specific situations.
- Skinnerians view personality development as a lifelong process in which response tendencies are shaped by reinforcement.

Bandura's theory

- Albert Bandura's *social cognitive theory* emphasizes how cognitive factors shape personality.
- According to Bandura, people's response tendencies are largely acquired through *observational learning*.
- Bandura stressed the role of *self-efficacy*— one's belief about one's ability to perform behaviors that should lead to expected outcomes.

Mischel's theory

- Walter Mischel's brand of social learning theory emphasizes how people behave differently in different situations.
- His theory has sparked debate about the relative importance of the person versus the situation in determining behavior.

Humanistic Perspectives

Rogers's theory

- Carl Rogers's *person-centered theory* focuses on the *self-concept*—a collection of subjective beliefs about one's nature.
- *Incongruence* is the degree of disparity between one's self-concept and one's actual experiences.
- According to Rogers, unconditional love during childhood fosters congruence while conditional love fosters incongruence.
- Rogers asserts that people with highly incongruent self-concepts are prone to recurrent anxiety.

Maslow's theory

- Abraham Maslow proposed that human motives are organized into a *hierarchy of needs*, in which basic needs must be met before less basic needs are aroused.
- At the top of Maslow's hierarchy of needs is the *need for self-actualization*—the need to fulfill one's potential.
- According to Maslow, *self-actualizing persons* are people with very healthy personalities, marked by continued personal growth.

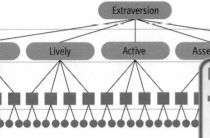

Extraversion

Lively   Active   Assertive

Eysenck's theory

- Hans Eysenck views personality structure as a hierarchy of traits in which many superficial traits are derived from a handful of fundamental traits.
- According to Eysenck, personality is largely determined by genetic inheritance.
- Eysenck theorizes that introversion and extraversion are shaped by inherited differences in arousability and ease of conditioning.

Behavioral genetics research

- Identical twins reared apart tend to be more similar in personality than fraternal twins reared together, which suggests that genetics shape personality.
- *Heritability estimates* for personality tend to hover around 40–50%.
- Behavioral genetics research has revealed that differences among families have surprisingly little impact on personality.

Biological Perspectives

The evolutionary approach

- Evolutionary analyses focus on how certain personality traits may have contributed to reproductive fitness in ancestral times.
- According to David Buss, the Big Five traits are especially important because they have had significant adaptive implications.

Culture and Personality

- Cross-cultural studies suggest that the basic trait structure of personality may be pancultural.
- American culture fosters an *independent view* of the self, whereas Asian cultures foster a more *interdependent view* of the self.

Agreeableness

Neuroticism   Conscientiousness

Extraversion   Openness to experience

Key Themes

- Psychology is theoretically diverse.
- Psychology evolves in a sociohistorical context.
- Behavior is shaped by cultural heritage.

Chapter 12

Stress, Coping, and Health

 Stress

 Stress Response

 Stress Effects

- *Stress* is a common, everyday event, and even routine hassles can have harmful effects.
- People's *appraisals* of events determine what they find stressful.

Major types of stress

Frustration

- *Frustration* occurs when the pursuit of some goal is thwarted.

Conflict

- In an *approach-approach conflict,* a choice must be made between two attractive goals.
- In an *avoidance-avoidance conflict,* a choice must be made between two unattractive alternatives.
- In an *approach-avoidance conflict,* a choice must be made about whether to pursue a goal that has positive and negative aspects.

Change

- *Life changes* are alterations in living circumstances, including positive changes, that require adjustment.
- The Social Readjustment Rating Scale (SRRS) purports to measure change-related stress, but actually taps many types of stressful experiences.
- Many studies have shown that high scores on the SRRS are associated with increased vulnerability to physical illness and psychological problems.

Pressure

- People may be put under *pressure* to perform well or to conform to others' expectations.
- Pressure is a predictor of psychological symptoms.

Emotional responses

- Many emotions may be evoked by stress, but anger-rage, anxiety-fear, and sadness-grief are especially common.
- Emotional arousal may interfere with coping efforts.
- The *inverted-U hypothesis* posits that as tasks become more complex, the optimal level of arousal decreases.

Physiological responses

- The *general adaptation syndrome* is Hans Selye's model of the body's response to stress, which can progress through three stages: alarm, resistance, and exhaustion.
- Stress can cause the brain to send signals to the endocrine system along two pathways.

Hypothalamus	Hypothalamus
↓	↓
Pituitary gland	**Autonomic nervous system**
↓	↓
Adrenal cortex	**Adrenal medulla**
↓	↓
Secretion of corticosteroids	**Secretion of catecholamines**

Behavioral responses

- Coping efforts may be healthy or unhealthy.
- *Giving up* and *blaming oneself* are less than optimal methods of coping with stress.
- Another unhealthy response is to strike out at others with acts of *aggression*.
- *Indulging oneself* is another common response to stress that tends to be less than optimal.
- *Defensive coping* protects against emotional distress, but it depends on self-deception and avoidance.
- However, several lines of research suggest that small positive illusions may be adaptive for mental health.
- *Constructive coping* refers to relatively healthful efforts to handle the demands of stress.

Effects on physical health

- Stress appears to contribute to many types of physical illness and not just *psychosomatic diseases*.
- *Type A behavior* has been identified as a contributing factor in coronary heart disease.
- Research suggests that *hostility* may be the most toxic element of the Type A syndrome.
- Recent evidence suggests that strong emotional reactions may precipitate heart attacks.
- Research indicates that depression is a predictor of heart disease.
- The association between stress and vulnerability to many diseases may reflect the negative impact of stress on immune function.
- The correlation between stress and illness is modest in strength because stress is only one of many factors that influence health.

Variations in stress tolerance

- There are individual differences in how much stress people can tolerate without negative effects.
- Strong *social support* and *optimism* are two factors that appear to increase people's stress tolerance.

Smoking

- Smokers have much higher mortality rates than nonsmokers because smoking elevates the risk for a wide range of diseases, including lung cancer and heart disease.
- When people quit smoking, their health risks decline fairly quickly and are noticeably lower after 5-7 years.
- Long-term success rates for giving up smoking are only 25% or less.

Lack of exercise

- Research indicates that regular exercise is associated with increased longevity.
- Physical fitness can reduce vulnerability to deadly cardiovascular diseases, obesity-related problems, and some types of cancer.

Health-Impairing Behavior

Poor nutritional habits

- Consumption of foods that elevate serum cholesterol and low-fiber diets appear to increase the risk of heart disease.
- High-fat and low-fiber diets have been implicated as possible contributors to some types of cancer.
- Chronic overeating contributes to obesity, which increases one's risk for heart disease, stroke, and other diseases.

Behavior and AIDS

- Behavioral patterns influence one's risk for AIDS, which is transmitted through person-to-person contact involving the exchange of bodily fluids, primarily semen and blood.
- In the world as a whole, sexual transmission has mostly taken place through heterosexual relations.
- Many people harbor unrealistic fears that AIDS can be readily transmitted through casual contact with infected individuals.
- Many young heterosexuals foolishly downplay their risk for HIV.

Reactions to Illness

The decision to seek treatment

- Whether people view physical sensations as symptoms of illness depends on subjective interpretation.
- The biggest problem in regard to treatment seeking is the common tendency to delay the pursuit of needed treatment.
- People procrastinate because they worry about looking silly or bothering their physician, or because they are reluctant to disrupt their plans.

Communicating with health providers

- About half of patients depart medical visits not understanding what they have been told.
- Barriers to effective provider-patient communication include short visits, overuse of medical jargon, and patients' reluctance to challenge physicians' authority.
- The key to improving communication is to not be a passive consumer.

Adherence to medical advice

- Nonadherence to advice from health providers is very common
- Nonadherence is often due to the patient's failure to understand instructions
- If a prescribed regimen is unpleasant or difficult to follow, compliance tends to decline.
- Noncompliance increases when patients have negative attitudes toward their health providers.

Key Themes

 Behavior is determined by multiple causes.

 People's experience of the world is highly subjective.

Chapter 13

Psychological Disorders

Abnormal Behavior

The medical model

- The *medical model*, which assumes that it is useful to view abnormal behavior as a disease, led to more humane treatment for people who exhibited abnormal behavior.
- However, the medical model has been criticized on the grounds that it converts moral and social questions into medical questions.

Criteria of abnormality

- Judgments of abnormality are based on three criteria: deviance from social norms, maladaptive behavior, and reports of personal distress.
- Normality and abnormality exist on a continuum.

The diagnostic system

- DSM-IV, which was released in 1994, is the official psychodiagnostic classification system in the United States.
- In DSM-IV information on patients is recorded on five axes: (I) clinical syndromes, (II) personality disorders, (III) general medical conditions, (IV) psychosocial stressors, and (V) global assessment of functioning.

Anxiety Disorders

Types

- *Generalized anxiety disorder* is marked by chronic, high anxiety not tied to a specific threat.
- *Phobic disorder* is marked by a peristent, irrational fear of an object or situation that is not dangerous.
- *Panic disorder* involves recurrent, sudden anxiety attacks, and is often accompanied by agoraphobia.
- *Obsessive-compulsive disorder* is marked by uncontrollable intrusions of unwanted thoughts and urges to engage in senseless rituals.
- *Posttraumatic stress disorder* involves enduring psychological disturbance attributable to the experience of a major traumatic event.

Etiology

- Twin studies suggest that there is a genetic predispostion to anxiety disorders.
- Disturbances in the neural circuits using GABA may play a role in some anxiety disorders.
- Many anxiety responses may be acquired through classical conditioning and maintained through operant conditioning.
- Cognitive theorists assert that the tendency to overinterpret harmless situations as threatening leads to anxiety disorders.
- High neuroticism and exposure to great stress may contribute to the emergence of some anxiety disorders.

Somatoform Disorders

Types

- *Somatization disorder* is marked by a history of diverse physical complaints that seem to be psychological in origin.
- *Conversion disorder* involves a significant loss of physical function with no apparent organic basis, usually in a single organ system.
- *Hypochondria* is marked by excessive preoccupation with one's health and constant worry about getting ill.

Etiology

- Cognitive theorists assert that people with somatoform disorders focus excessive attention on bodily sensations and apply an unrealistic standard of good health.
- Somatoform disorders may occur in people who learn to like the sick role because it allows them to avoid stress and gain sympathy.

Dissociative Disorders

Types

- *Dissociative amnesia* is a sudden loss of memory for personal information that is too extensive to be due to normal forgetting.
- In *dissociative fugue,* people lose their memory for their entire lives along with their sense of identity.
- *Dissociative identity disorder* (or multiple personality disorder) involves the coexistence of two or more largely complete and usually very different personalities.

Etiology

- Dissociative amnesia and fugue are usually attributed to extreme stress.
- Some theorists maintain that people with dissociative identity disorder are engaging in intentional role-playing to use mental illness as an excuse for their personal failings.
- Other theorists maintain that cases of dissociative identity disorder are rooted in severe emotional trauma that occurred during childhood.

Mood Disorders

Types

- *Major depressive disorder* is marked by persistent feelings of sadness and despair, loss of interest in previous sources of pleasure, slowed thought processes, and self-blame.
- *Bipolar disorder* (manic-depressive disorder) is marked by the experience of depressed and manic episodes, with the latter involving irrational euphoria, racing thoughts, impulsive behavior, and increased energy.

Etiology

- Twin studies suggest that there is a genetic predispostion to mood disorders.
- Disturbances in the neural circuits using serotonin and norepinephrine appear to contribute to mood disorders.
- Cognitive theorists assert that people who exhibit a pessimistic explanatory style are especially vulnerable to depression and that rumination tends to extend and amplify episodes of depression.
- Behavioral theories emphasize how inadequate social skills increase vulnerability to depression.
- High stress is associated with increased vulnerability to mood disorders.

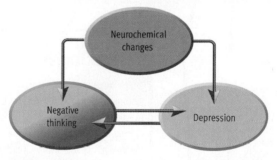

Neurochemical changes → Negative thinking → Depression

Culture and Pathology

- The *relativistic view* holds that the criteria of mental illness vary considerably across cultures.
- The *pancultural view* holds that the criteria of mental illness are much the same around the world.
- Research indicates that serious mental disorders are identifiable in all cultures, but there are cultural variations in the recognition of less severe forms of disturbance.

Schizophrenic Disorders

General symptoms and subtypes

- The general symptoms of schizophrenia include irrational thought, delusions, deterioration of adaptive behavior, distorted perception, hallucinations, and disturbed emotion.
- *Paranoid schizophrenia* is dominated by delusions of persecution and delusions of grandeur.
- *Catatonic schizophrenia* is marked by striking motor disturbances, ranging from muscular rigidity to random motor activity.
- *Disorganized schizophrenia* is marked by very severe deterioration of adaptive behavior.
- *Undifferentiated schizophrenia* is marked by idiosyncratic mixtures of schizophrenic symptoms.
- Some theorists have proposed dividing schizophrenic disorders into two categories based on the dominance of *negative symptoms* (behavioral deficits) versus *positive symptoms* (behavioral excesses and peculiarities).
- Factors associated with a favorable prognosis include sudden onset of the disease at a later age, good social adjustment, a low proportion of negative symptoms, and a supportive family.

Etiology

- Twin studies and adoption studies suggest that there is a genetic vulnerability to schizophrenia.
- Disturbances at dopamine synapses have been implicated as a possible cause of schizophrenia.
- Research has uncovered an association between enlarged brain ventricles and schizophrenic disturbance.
- The neurodevelopmental hypothesis posits that vulnerability to schizophrenia is increased by disruptions of the normal maturational processes of the brain during prenatal development or at birth.
- Schizophrenic patients from families high in expressed emotion have elevated relapse rates.
- High stress is associated with increased vulnerability to schizophrenic disorders.

Key Themes

 Psychology evolves in a sociohistorical context.

Heredity and environment jointly influence behavior.

 Behavior is shaped by cultural heritage.

Behavior is determined by multiple causes.

Chapter 14

Treatment of Psychological Disorders

Elements of Treatment

Treatment approaches

Insight therapies

Behavior therapies

Biomedical therapies

Insight Therapies

Psychoanalysis

- Sigmund Freud believed that neuroses are caused by *unconscious conflicts* regarding sex and aggression left over from childhood.
- In psychoanalysis, *dream analysis* and *free association* are used to explore the unconscious.
- When an analyst's *interpretations* touch on sensitive issues *resistance* can be expected.
- The *transference* relationship may be used to overcome resistance and promote insight.

Client-centered therapy

- According to Carl Rogers, neurotic anxieties are due to *incongruence* between one's self-concept and reality.
- Rogers maintained that the *process* of therapy is not as crucial as the therapeutic *climate*.
- To create a healthy climate therapists must be genuine, and provide unconditional positive regard and empathy.
- The key process at work in client-centered therapy is the *clarification* of clients' feelings.

Group therapy

- Most insight therapies can be conducted on a group basis, which involves the simultaneous treatment of several or more clients.
- In group therapy, participants essentially function as therapists for one another as they share experiences, coping strategies, and support.
- Group therapists usually play a subtle role, staying in the background and working to promote group cohesiveness and supportive interactions.

Evaluating insight therapies

- Evaluating the effectiveness of any approach to treatment is extremely complicated and subjective.
- Nonetheless, hundreds of outcome studies collectively suggest that insight therapy is superior to placebo treatment and that the beneficial effects of therapy are reasonably durable.
- *Common factors* may account for some of the progress that clients make in insight therapies.

Behavior Therapies

General principles

- Behaviorists assume that even pathological behavior is a product of learning and that what has been learned can be unlearned.
- In behavior therapy, specific procedures are designed to treat specific problems.

Systematic desensitization

Joseph Wolpe's systematic desensitization, a treatment for phobias, involves the construction of an anxiety hierarchy, relaxation training, and movement through the hierarchy pairing relaxation with each phobic stimulus.

Cognitive-Behavioral treatments

- Cognitive therapy was devised as a treatment for depression, but is now used for a variety of disorders.
- Aaron Beck asserts that most disorders are caused by irrational, rigid, negative thinking.
- The goal of cognitive therapy is to help clients learn to detect and dispute their automatic negative thoughts.

Therapists

Clinical and *counseling psychologists* specialize in the diagnosis and treatment of mental disorders and everyday problems.

Psychiatric social workers, psychiatric nurses, and *counselors* also provide psychotherapy services.

Psychiatrists are physicians who specialize in the diagnosis and treatment of mental disorders.

Clients

- About 15% of the U. S. population uses mental health services each year, although about half of these do not have a specific disorder.
- People vary in their willingness to seek therapy and many who need therapy don't receive it.

Biomedical Therapies

Drug treatments

- *Antianxiety drugs,* which are used to relieve nervousness, are effective in the short term, but have potential for abuse, dependence, and overdose.
- *Antipsychotic drugs* can gradually reduce psychotic symptoms, but they have many unpleasant side effects.
- *Antidepressant drugs* can gradually relieve episodes of depression, but even the newer SSRIs are not free of side effects.
- *Lithium* and other *mood stabilizers* can help to prevent future episodes of both mania and depression in bipolar patients.
- Drug therapies can lead to impressive positive effects, but critics worry that drugs produce short-lived gains, are overprescribed, and more dangerous than widely appreciated.
- Critics also argue that conflicts of interest are a pervasive problem in research on new medications, leading to overestimates of drugs' efficacy and underestimates of their negative side effects.

Social skills training

Social skills training is designed to improve clients' interpersonal interactions through modeling, behavioral rehearsal, and shaping.

Aversion therapy

In aversion therapy, a stimulus that elicits an unwanted response is paired with something unpleasant in an effort to eliminate the maladaptive response.

Electroconvulsive therapy

- In *electroconvulsive therapy (ECT),* electric shock is used to produce a cortical seizure and convulsions which are believed to be useful in the treatment of depression.
- Proponents of ECT maintain that it is a very effective treatment, but critics have raised doubts and only about 8% of psychiatrists use ECT.
- Memory losses are a short-term side effect of ECT, but there is great debate about whether ECT carries significant long-term risks.

Institutional Treatment in Transition

Current Issues in Treatment

- Critics argue that managed care has restricted access to mental health care and reduced its quality and length.
- One positive response to the demands of managed care has been to increase research efforts to validate the efficacy of specific treatments for specific problems.
- The culture-bound origins of Western therapies have raised doubts about their applicability to other cultures and even to ethnic groups in Western societies.
- Ethnic minorities in America underutilize mental health services because of cultural distrust, language difficulties, and institutional barriers.

- Disenchantment with traditional mental hospitals led to the *community mental health movement,* which advocates local, community-based care and prevention of mental disorders.
- *Deinstitutionalization* refers to the transfer of mental health care from inpatient institutions to community-based outpatient facilities.
- Deinstitutionalization has contributed to the *revolving door problem,* which refers to the frequent, readmission of patients suffering from severe disorders.
- Deinstitutionalization has also contributed to the growth of homelessness, and the increased incidence of mental illness among the homeless, although homelessness is primarily an economic problem.

Key Themes

- Psychology is theoretically diverse
- Behavior is shaped by cultural heritage

Chapter 15

Social Behavior

Person Perception

- Judgments of others can be distorted by their physical appearance, as we tend to ascribe desirable personality characteristics and competence to those who are good looking.
- *Social schemas* and *stereotypes* can influence our perceptions of others.
- Stereotypes tend to be broad overgeneralizations that can lead us to see what we expect to see and to overestimate how often we have seen it (the *illusory correlation* effect).
- People tend to overestimate the degree to which others pay attention to them (the *spotlight effect*), and people tend to think that their knowledge of their peers is greater than their peers' knowledge of them (the *illusion of asymmetric insight*).
- Evolutionary psychologists argue that many biases in person perception, such as the tendency to quickly categorize people into *ingroups* and *outgroups,* exist because they were adaptive in humans' ancestral past.

Attribution

Basic processes

- *Attributions* are inferences that people draw about the causes of events and behaviors.
- *Internal attributions* ascribe the causes of behavior to personal traits, abilities, and feelings, whereas *external attributions* ascribe the causes of behavior to situational demands and environmental factors.
- According to Bernard Weiner, attributions for success and failure can be analyzed along the stable-unstable and internal-external dimensions.

Biases

- The *fundamental attribution error* refers to observers' bias in favor of internal attributions in explaining others' behavior.
- Actors favor external attributions in explaining their own behavior, whereas observers favor internal attributions.
- The *self-serving bias* is the tendency to explain one's successes with internal attributions and one's failures with external attributions.

Cultural influences

- Cultures vary in their emphasis on *individualism* (putting personal goals ahead of group goals) as opposed to *collectivism* (putting group goals ahead of personal goals), which influence attributional tendencies.
- People from collectivist cultures appear to be less prone to the fundamental attribution error and to the self-serving bias than people from individualist cultures.

Interpersonal Attraction

Factors in attraction

- A key determinant of romantic attraction for both sexes is physical attractiveness.
- The *matching hypothesis* asserts that males and females of roughly equal physical attractiveness are likely to select each other as partners.
- Married and dating couples tend to be similar on many traits, probably because similarity causes attraction and because attraction can foster similarity.
- Research on *reciprocity* shows that liking breeds liking and that loving promotes loving.
- In romantic relationships people evaluate how close their partners come to matching their ideals, but these perceptions are highly subjective, so partners often come to idealize each other.

Cultural and evolutionary influences

- The traits that people seek in prospective mates seem to transcend culture, but societies vary in their emphasis on romantic love as a prerequisite for marriage.
- According to evolutionary psychologists, some aspects of good looks influence attraction because they have been indicators of reproductive fitness.
- Men tend to be more interested than women in seeking youthfulness and attractiveness in mates, whereas women tend to emphasize potential mates' financial prospects.
- The gender gap in mating priorities influences the tactics that men and women use in pursuing romantic relationships.
- Women tend to underestimate men's relationship commitment, whereas men tend to overestimate women's sexual interest.

Perspectives on love

- Some theorists distinguish between *passionate love* and *companionate love*, with the latter divisible into *intimacy* and *commitment*.
- Another approach views romantic love as an *attachment process* and argues that love relationships in adulthood mimic attachment patterns in infancy, which fall into three categories: secure, anxious-ambivalent, and avoidant.

Attitudes

The structure of attitudes

Components

- The *cognitive component* of an attitude is made up of the beliefs that people hold about the object of an attitude.
- The *affective component* of an attitude consists of the emotional feelings stimulated by an object of thought.
- The *behavioral component* of an attitude consists of predispositions to act in certain ways towards an attitudinal object.

Dimensions

- *Attitude strength* refers to how firmly attitudes are held.
- *Attitude accessibility* refers to how often and how quickly an attitude comes to mind.
- *Attitude ambivalence* refers to how conflicted one feels about an attitude.

Trying to change attitudes

Source factors

- Persuasion tends to be more successful when a source has credibility, which may depend on expertise or trustworthiness.
- Likability also tends to increase success in persuasion.

Message factors

- Two-sided arguments tend to be more effective than one-sided presentations.
- Fear appeals tend to work if they are actually successful in arousing fear.

Receiver factors

- Persuasion is more difficult when the receiver is forewarned about the persuasive effort.
- Resistance is greater when a message is incompatible with the receiver's existing attitudes and when strong attitudes are targeted.

Theories of attitude change

Learning theory

- The affective component of an attitude can be shaped by classical conditioning.
- Attitudes can be strengthened by reinforcement or acquired through observational learning.

Dissonance theory

- According to Leon Festinger, inconsistency between attitudes motivates attitude change.
- Dissonance theory can explain attitude change after counter-attitudinal behavior or when people need to justify their great effort to attain something.

Elaboration likelihood model

- The *central route* to persuasion depends on the logic of one's message, whereas the *peripheral route* depends on nonmessage factors, such as emotions.
- Research indicates that the central route produces more durable attitude change.

Yielding to Others

Conformity

- Research by Solomon Asch showed that people have a surprisingly strong tendency to conform.
- Asch found that conformity becomes more likely as group size increases up to a point.
- However, the presence of another dissenter in a group greatly reduces the conformity observed.
- Asch's findings have been replicated in many cultures, with even higher levels of conformity observed in collectivist societies.

Obedience

- In Stanley Milgram's landmark study, adult men drawn from the community showed a remarkable tendency to follow orders to shock an innocent stranger, with 65% delivering the maximum shock.
- The generalizability of Milgram's findings has stood the test of time, but his work helped stimulate stricter ethical standards for research.
- Milgram's findings have been replicated in many modern nations and even higher rates of obedience have been seen in many places.

Behavior in Groups

- The *bystander effect* refers to the fact that people are less likely to provide help when they are in groups than when they are alone, because of diffusion of responsibility.
- Productivity often declines in groups because of loss of coordination and *social loafing,* which refers to the reduced effort seen when people work in groups.
- *Group polarization* occurs when discussion leads a group to shift toward a more extreme decision in the direction it was already leaning.
- In *groupthink,* a cohesive group suspends critical thinking in a misguided effort to promote agreement.

Key Themes

 Psychology is empirical.

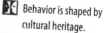 Behavior is shaped by cultural heritage.

 People's experience of the world is highly subjective.

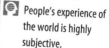 Behavior is determined by multiple causes.

Notes

Notes

Notes